WHICH IS WORSE?

By Lee Taylor

CRAZY QUESTIONS TO ASK YOUR FRIENDS!

SCHOLASTIC INC.

ISBN 978-1-338-04304-4

10 9 8 7 6 5 4 3   17 18 19 20 21

Printed in the U.S.A.   40
First edition, January 2017

Cover design by Liz Frances
Interior design by Kay Petronio

How do you choose between
horrible and horrendous?!
It's time to find out. Snag your friends,
grab a snack, and hunker down for more than
100 crazy questions that **MAKE** you choose.
Some are embarrassing, some are scary,
and some are totally gross.

But NONE of them are good.

So go ahead and choose . . .

WHICH ◄IS► WORSE???

WHICH IS WORSE

HAVING STINKY FEET

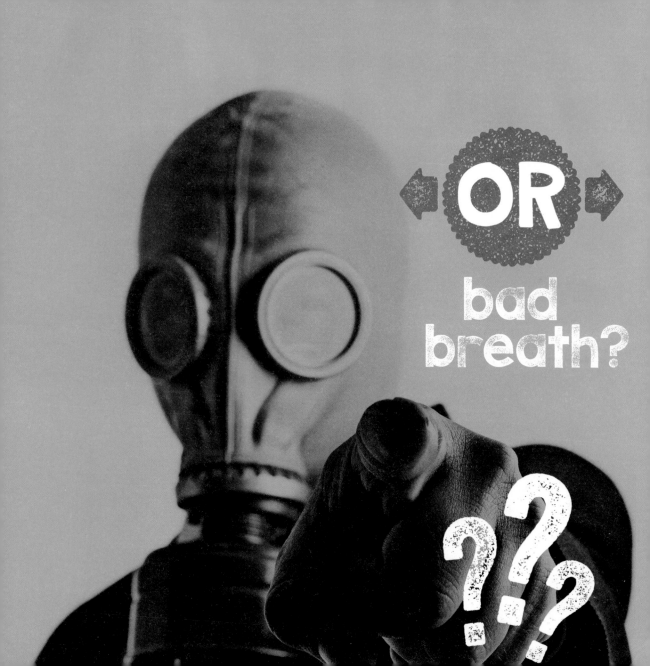

OR

bad breath?

??

SLEEPING IN A HAUNTED HOUSE FOR THE NIGHT

OR

SLEEPING IN YOUR OWN ROOM WITH SQUEAKY MICE?

WHICH IS WORSE

MEALWORMS IN YOUR FACE WASH ◄ OR ► MEALWORMS IN YOUR BODY WASH?

ALWAYS SMELLING LIKE ROTTEN EGGS

OR

LIKE YOU NEVER WEAR DEODORANT?

WHICH IS WORSE

HAVING FOOD STUCK IN YOUR TEETH ALL DAY

◀OR▶

DROOLING
EVERY TIME
YOU TALK?

WHICH IS WORSE

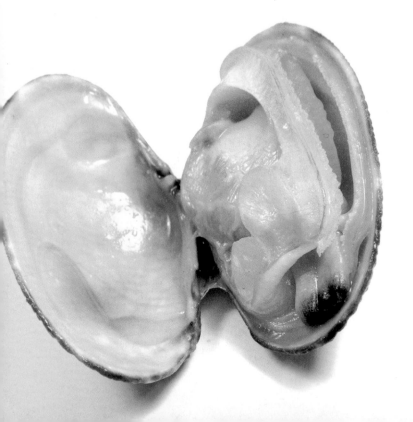

drinking
a glass
of clam
juice

OR → a glass of pig slop?

???

OR

LIMA BEAN WAFFLES? ???

WHICH IS WORSE

BEING STRUCK BY LIGHTNING

OR

GETTING CAUGHT IN AN AVALANCHE?

WHICH IS WORSE

GETTING CALLED TO THE PRINCIPAL'S OFFICE  **OR** THROWING UP DURING AN ASSEMBLY?

STEPPING IN COW PATTIES

OR

FALLING INTO A PIGSTY?

WHICH IS WORSE

IS

licking a clean slug

OR licking a dirty spoon? ???

OR

A GIANT SQUID?

WHICH IS WORSE

BEING CHASED BY A ZOMBIE HORDE

OR

ABDUCTED BY ALIENS?

???

OR a shark?

OR

???

getting sprayed by a skunk?

WHICH IS WORSE

SWIMMING AWAY FROM THE LOCH NESS MONSTER

WHICH IS WORSE

one thousand tiny ants in your kitchen

OR one humongous ant in your bedroom?

WHICH IS WORSE

being lost in a mummy-filled museum

OR → trapped in a killer-robot factory?

WHICH IS WORSE

BEING CLOGGED UP WITH A LOT OF SNOT

 OR

A LOT OF EARWAX?

WHICH IS WORSE

EATING ROTTEN-MEAT STEW

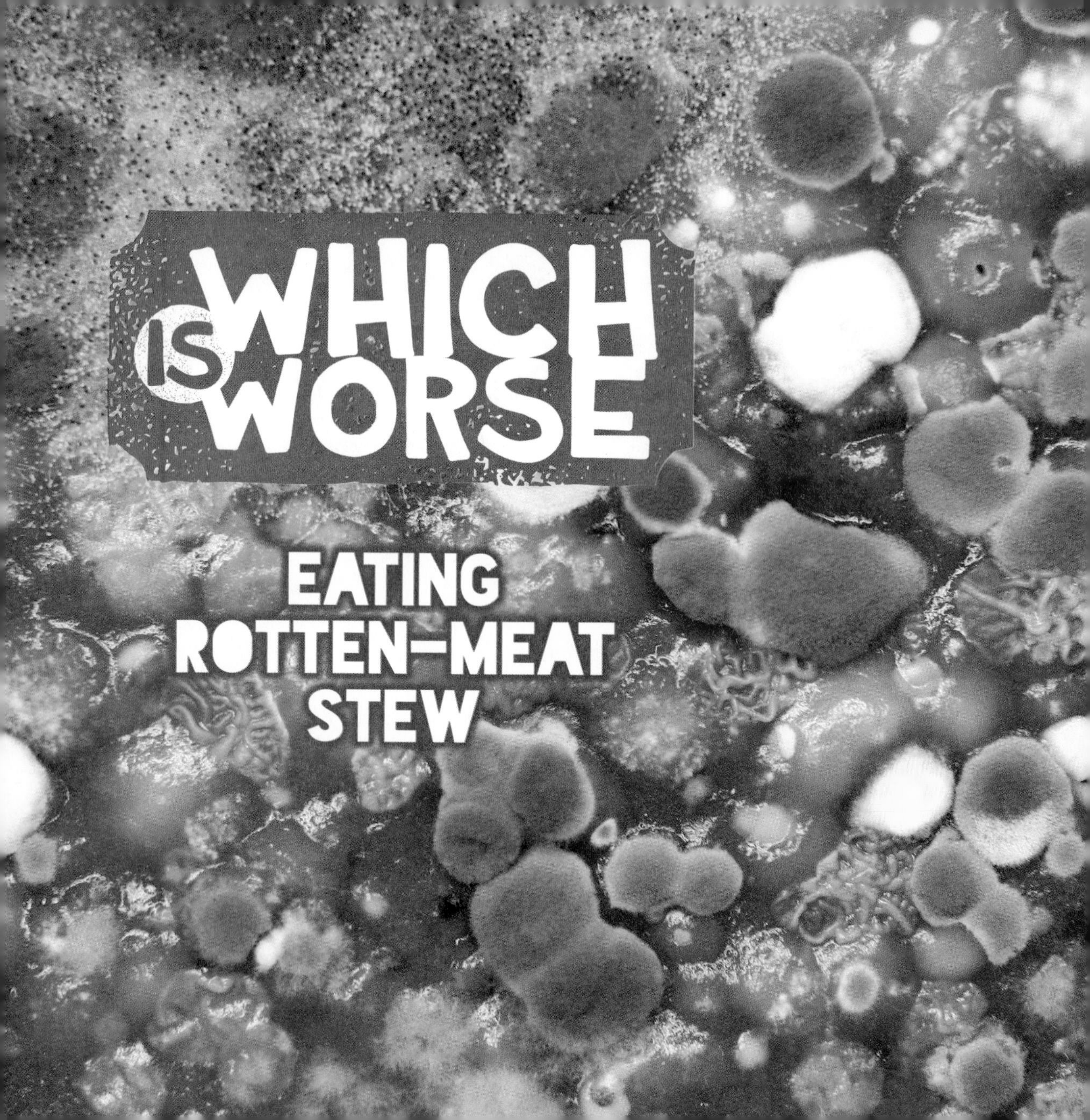

◀ **OR** ▶

ROADKILL CASSEROLE?

WHICH IS WORSE

REALIZING THERE WAS A WORM IN YOUR APPLE

OR

FINDING OUT THE CRUNCHY CANDY YOU JUST ATE WAS A CHOCOLATE-COVERED COCKROACH?

WHICH IS WORSE

your phone battery dying in the middle of your favorite band's concert

OR

right before
spotting your
favorite celeb?

WHICH WORSE

BEING CAPTURED BY PIRATES

GETTING THROWN OVERBOARD INTO SHARK-INFESTED WATERS?

WHICH IS WORSE

SWIMMING IN GARBAGE

OR

SWIMMING WITH ELECTRIC EELS?

WHICH IS WORSE

a bite from a rattlesnake

OR

a sting from a scorpion?

WHICH IS WORSE

SUPERGLUING YOUR HANDS TOGETHER

OR

???

WASHING YOUR FACE WITH HOT SAUCE?

WHICH IS WORSE

snacking on maggots OR dung beetles?

BEING LOCKED IN AN OLD PORTA-POTTY

OR

GETTING STUCK ON A STINKY FISHING BOAT?

WHICH IS WORSE

BEING STUCK IN THE DESERT WITHOUT WATER

◄ OR ►

ADRIFT IN THE OCEAN WITHOUT A LIFE RAFT?

WHICH IS WORSE

A RAT STEALING YOUR SNACK

OR

A RAT
WALKING ALL
OVER YOUR
SNACK?

WHICH IS WORSE

hearing mysterious footsteps in the attic at night

OR

a ghostly moan outside your window?

???

OR SAILING ON THE TITANIC?

WHICH IS WORSE

running out of
oxygen underwater

OR

in outer
space?

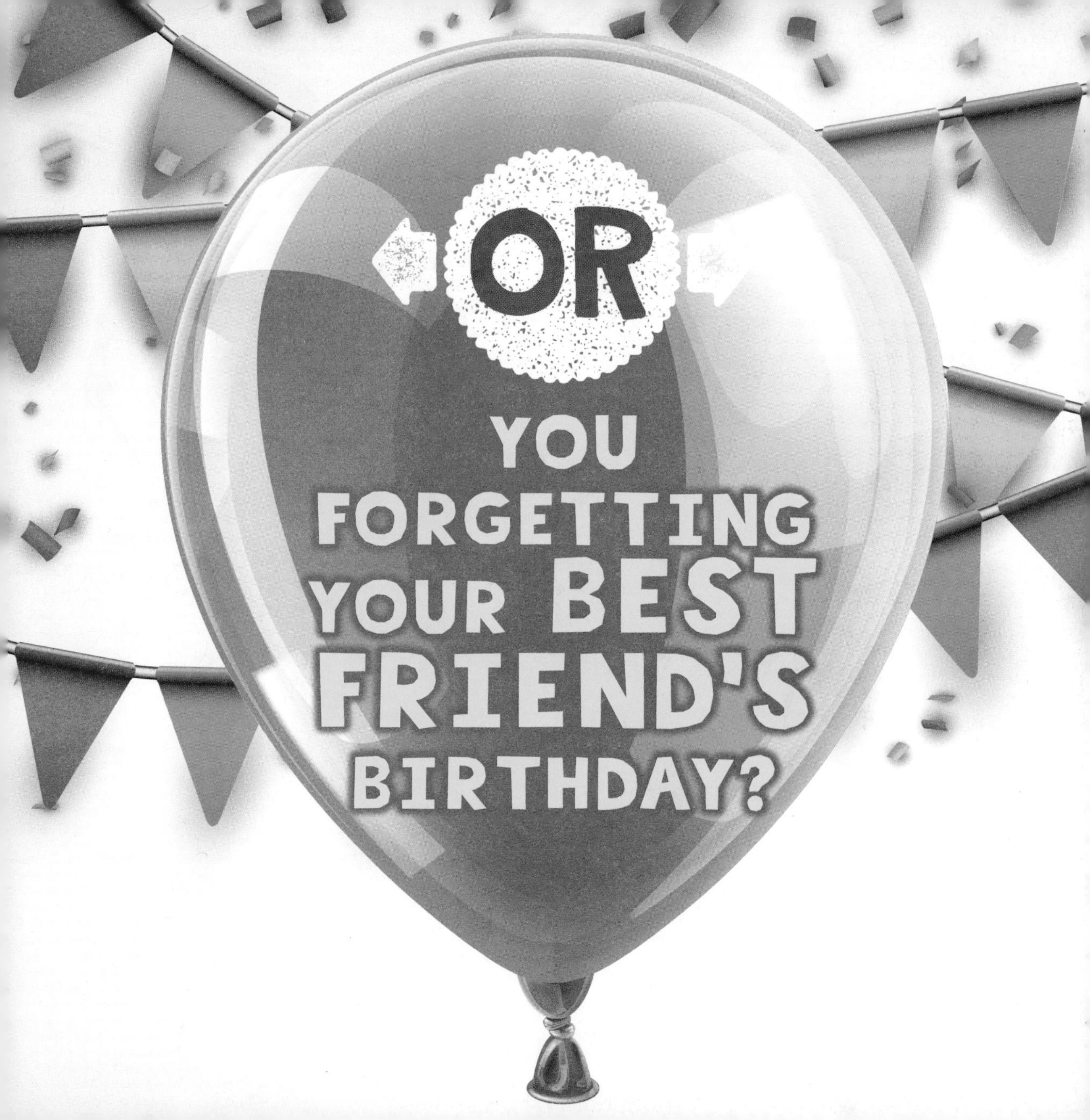
OR
YOU FORGETTING YOUR BEST FRIEND'S BIRTHDAY?

WHICH IS WORSE

BEING ATTACKED BY A SWARM OF KILLER BEES

OR

A SCHOOL OF PIRANHAS?

WHICH IS WORSE eating a cup of mayonnaise

OR

chugging a cup
of raw eggs?

??

WHICH IS WORSE

being haunted by ghosts

OR

becoming a ghost?

GETTING BITTEN BY A WEREWOLF  A VAMPIRE?

WHICH IS WORSE

SITTING ON AN EXPLODING TOILET

OR

CLIMBING COLLAPSING STAIRS?

WHICH IS WORSE

TAKING A BATH IN FROGS' EGGS

◀ OR ▶

A SKUNK-SPRAY SHOWER???

WHICH IS WORSE

getting stuck in
the Jurassic Era

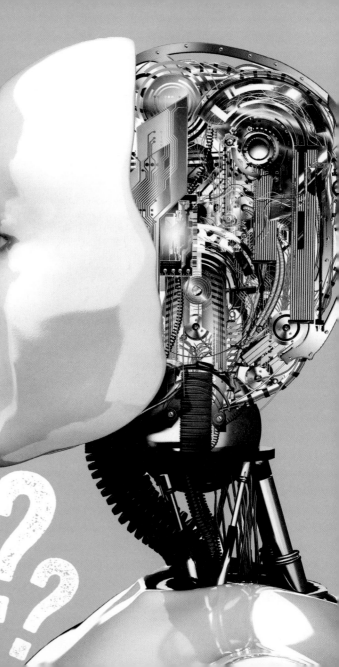

OR

stuck
in the
future
when
robots
are in
charge? **???**

WHICH IS WORSE

being stranded on a desert island

OR

stuck on a mountain?

WHICH IS WORSE

HAVING A BABOON'S BUTT

OR

A PORCUPINE'S HAIR?

WHICH IS WORSE

BEING THE FIRST ZOMBIE
OF THE ZOMBIE APOCALYPSE

OR THE LAST HUMAN LEFT?

OR

AN ENTIRE
YEAR OF
NIGHTMARES?

WHICH IS WORSE

having
24 hours of
sunlight

OR 24 hours of total darkness? ???

WHICH IS WORSE

being buried alive ◄ OR ► sunk at sea?

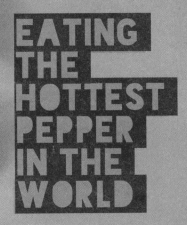

EATING
THE
HOTTEST
PEPPER
IN THE
WORLD

OR

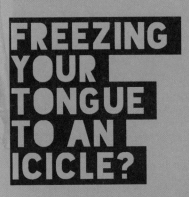

FREEZING
YOUR
TONGUE
TO AN
ICICLE?

WHICH IS WORSE

BEING THE LAST PERSON ON EARTH

WHICH IS WORSE

drinking
a glass
of toilet
water

OR ⬅ ➡ eating a rotten egg?

???

WHICH IS WORSE

wearing your
grandma's
dentures

OR

your uncle's toupee?

WHICH IS WORSE

getting woken up by an air horn going off in your ear

OR

by a bucket of ice water
dumped on your head?

WHICH IS WORSE

being transformed into a dirty toilet

OR a baby's diaper?

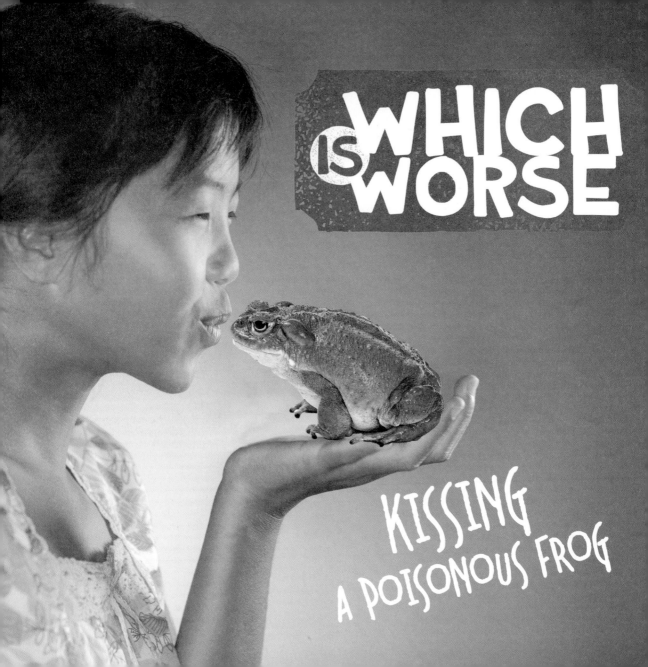

WHICH IS WORSE

KISSING A POISONOUS FROG

OR FLOSSING A CROCODILE'S TEETH?

WHICH IS WORSE

a family of
millipedes
crawling
on your
hairbrush

OR

a smelly stinkbug crawling on your toothbrush?

WHICH IS WORSE

IS

falling into a sinkhole

◀ OR ▶

being sucked into a tornado?

WHICH IS WORSE

having cavities ← OR → warts?

BEING CHASED BY A RABID SQUIRREL

OR

FOLLOWED BY A BUZZING SWARM OF MOSQUITOES?

WHICH IS WORSE

FARTING RIGHT BEFORE YOUR CRUSH ENTERS THE ROOM

OR IN THE MIDDLE OF A QUIET MOVIE THEATER?

WHICH IS WORSE

WALKING AROUND WITH TOILET PAPER STUCK TO YOUR SHOE

OR **wITH YOUR zIPPER DOWN?**

WHICH IS WORSE

FALLING INTO A PIT FULL OF BOA CONSTRICTORS

◄**OR**► **A POOL FULL OF STINGING JELLYFISH?**

WHICH IS WORSE

a bird pooping on your head

OR stepping in dog poop?

???

WHICH IS WORSE

HAVING A MOUTHFUL OF FISH SCALES

WHICH IS WORSE

WATCHING A SCARY MOVIE IN THE DARK

OR

GETTING
LOCKED IN
A CREEPY
BASEMENT?

???

WHICH IS WORSE

living in a world before smartphones

OR

before indoor toilets?

WHICH IS WORSE

HAVING NEVER-ENDING DIARRHEA

OR

NEVER-ENDING
VOMITING?

WHICH IS WORSE

Sitting in a seat
with gum on it

OR

Sitting in a seat with
a mystery puddle?

WHICH IS WORSE

having all your hair fall out OR having all your teeth fall out?

WHICH IS WORSE

GETTING A
SLUG-SLIME FACIAL

OR

A MOTOR OIL MASSAGE?

WHICH IS WORSE

no Internet

OR no video games?

WHICH IS WORSE

eating a skunk burger for dinner

a snake-egg omelet for breakfast?

WHICH IS WORSE

being sucked into a horror movie

OR

the villain
coming
out into
the real
world?

WHICH IS WORSE

getting
amnesia and
forgetting your
crush

OR your crush getting amnesia and forgetting you?

WHICH IS WORSE

using toenails as ice cream sprinkles

OR dandruff to season your fries?

OR

A SINKING BOAT?

???

WHICH IS WORSE

THROWING UP SLUGS

OR

SNEEZING OUT FLIES?

WHICH IS WORSE

BEING LOST AND ALONE IN THE DARK WOODS

OR

LOCKED IN A CROWDED ROOM?

GRAPE JELLY ON YOUR FRIES ◄ **OR** ► ORANGE JUICE IN YOUR CEREAL?

WHICH IS WORSE

wearing the same pair of underwear for the rest of your life

OR

the same
pair of
socks?

WHICH IS WORSE

forgetting your phone during a long family road trip

OR

being stuck on a long flight with a crying baby?

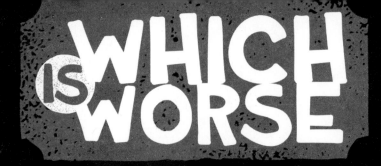

WHICH IS WORSE

Being

in the

Middle of a

Wildfire

OR a hurricane?

WHICH IS WORSE

HAVING A BLANKET
MADE OF HUMAN SKIN

OR A PILLOW STUFFED WITH HUMAN INTESTINES?

WHICH IS WORSE

HAVING TO SING EVERYTHING YOU SAY

never being able
to watch TV

only being able to
watch commercials?

WHICH IS WORSE

peeing your pants every time you laugh

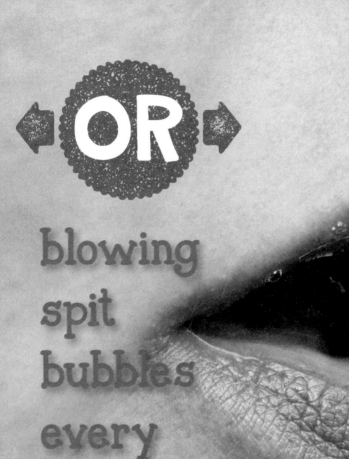

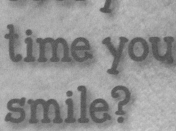
blowing
spit
bubbles
every
time you
smile?

WHICH IS WORSE

ONLY BEING
ABLE TO
LAUGH LIKE
A HYENA

OR

REPEATING THINGS LIKE A PARROT?

WHICH IS WORSE

eating a plate of brains OR a plate of eyeballs?

CEMETERY

SPENDING THE NIGHT IN A GRAVEYARD ◀ **OR** ▶ IN AN ABANDONED MINE SHAFT?

WHICH IS WORSE

Saying hello to
everyone you
meet by Sniffing
their butt

OR licking their face?

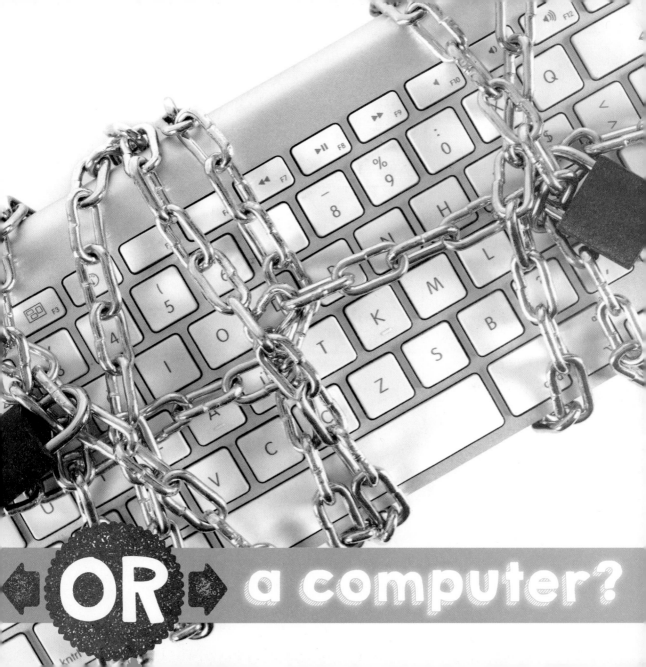

OR a computer?

WHICH IS WORSE

COUGHING UP HAIRBALLS

 **OR**

EATING GUM THAT HAS ALREADY BEEN CHEWED?

WHICH IS WORSE

plucking out all of your eyelashes

OR shaving off both of your eyebrows?

WHICH IS WORSE

having the diet of a vulture

OR

a dung beetle?

WHICH IS WORSE

ALWAYS HAVING TOE FUNGUS

OR PINKEYE?

WHICH IS WORSE

NEVER BEING ABLE TO FLUSH THE TOILET

WHICH IS WORSE

IS

having poison ivy all over your body

WHICH IS WORSE

WALKING BAREFOOT ACROSS A FIELD OF BROKEN GLASS **OR** A BED OF HOT COALS?

A SPELL THAT TURNS YOU INTO A BABY

OR

ONE THAT MAKES YOU SUPER OLD?

WHICH IS WORSE

USING SANDPAPER AS TOILET PAPER

OR USED TISSUES AS A TOWEL?

WHICH IS WORSE

bungee JUMPing into a geyseR

OR

SKYdiving in a Lightning STORM?

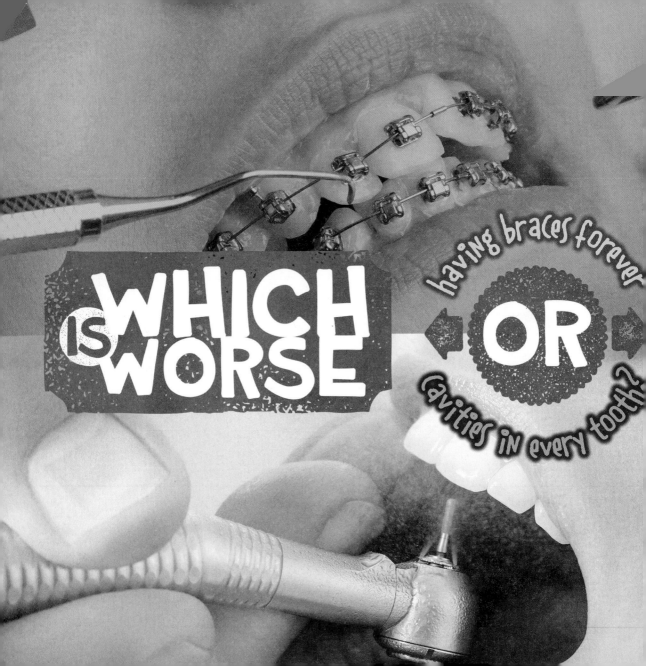

WHICH IS WORSE

having braces forever OR cavities in every tooth?

DRINKING A
POND-SCUM
MILKSHAKE  A GYM-SWEAT
SMOOTHIE?

WHICH IS WORSE

EATING A SUNDAE
TOPPED WITH
BLOOD

OR

BIRD
POOP?

PHOTO CREDITS